RASPBERRY PI 3
THE ONLY ESSENTIAL QUICK & EASY BOOK YOU NEED TO
START YOUR OWN RASPBERRY PROJECTS IMMEDIATELY

RASPBERRY PI PROGRAMMING
FOR BEGINNERS

RONALD OLSEN

AUVA PRESS

FIRST EDITION

ISBN-13: 978-1-5441-4145-9
ISBN-10: 1-5441-4145-9

Editor: Michelle Gabel
Cover Designer: Annie Eaves

To friendship and to my family,
who make my world more meaningful

Introduction

Every second of time something new is created on this world, whether only in our minds or in our hands. The Raspberry Pi 3 is a perfect example of how the technologies are rapidly changing.

Four years ago, since its first launching, Raspberry Pi ran a single core processor, and now it can run up to four core processor. It became ten times better than it was four years ago. Not just that, but the company has also taken a significant leap in upgrading the Raspberry Pi 3's network connection. Now, it has a built-in Bluetooth and Wi-Fi. Despite this big leap, the Raspberry Pi Foundation stays committed to its goal, to make it affordable for people who want to explore computers.

Well, you sure can do a lot using this mini-computer board. You can control robots and transform your dumb television into a smart one. You can also build a security system in your house or a theater for your room. Also, it can run a simple version of Minecraft for you, or maybe for your child to enjoy.

RONALD OLSEN

This book contains some easy to understand explanations in order to help you understand Raspberry Pi 3. It provides some basic instructions, such as how to install the things that need to be installed, like the NOOBS and the operating system. Additionally, it delivers some useful accessories you might need for your Raspberry Pi 3 and, of course, lists projects that you can do with it. Projects are ranging from entertainment to your home security, automation, robotics, and whatever it is that you like to create. The only limit is your imagination and determination.

CONTENTS

Chapter 1

Understanding Raspberry Pi 3

Raspberry Pi 3 is the third generation of the Raspberry Pis. It is a credit card-size single board computer. Its original purpose was to become an affordable platform for learning how to code, and applied in various electronic projects. Although the Raspberry Pi is just a 3x2 inch board, it has all the components that your typical computer needs. It has a System-on-Chip (SoC), or the brain of a computer, a GPU, power input, a CSI port to connect to your camera, a DSI Port, 40 GPIO pins, and four USB ports.

IS THIS BOOK FOR ME?

If you have bought a Raspberry Pi 3 and you are interested in exploring computers, then this book is perfect for you. It doesn't matter if you're a mom, a student, a professional, or even a beginner. This book is for anyone who wants to create something with his or her new Raspberry Pi 3.

Raspberry Pi 3, again, is a single-board computer that is set up by the Raspberry Pi Foundation, mainly to help children who want to learn programming languages like Scratch and Python. That is why they have created a cheap, affordable but useful, single board computer.

However, this book is not for children, because Raspberry Pi 3 is not limited to learning how to program. It can find an application in various disciplines. For that reason, whatever your interests might be, this book is for you.

WHAT CAN I EXPECT FROM THIS BOOK

This book contains sample projects you can execute with your Raspberry Pi 3. We have also included Raspberry Pi 3's specifications, explained in a simple manner so that even your kid can understand. We will also help you in setting up NOOBS installation, OS installation (Raspbian, Windows 10 IOT, OpenELEC, and Ubuntu MATE), and other important things in setting up a functional and working Raspberry Pi 3.

Our team created this book to help you start your Raspberry Pi project. We believe that your creativity can produce great things and we want to help you with that. Who knows? Maybe what you might accomplish is the next big thing in the technology business and we would be happy and would love to be part of it.

WHY RASPBERRY PI 3 AND NOT ANY OTHER SINGLE BOARD COMPUTER?

Four years ago, before the first ever launch of the Raspberry Pi, there weren't many low-cost single board computers running Linux. Additionally, the best of those single board computers were a bit expensive. Their cost was somewhere about $150. Raspberry Pi costs $35, functions equally well, and has the same specification as other expensive single board computers on the market.

It is not only affordable but is easy to use. Other single-board computers only run one program at a time, but Raspberry Pi has the ability to run multiple programs. If you compare it to the older generations of the Raspberry Pi's, it has gotten up to ten times better but still cost the same. That is why we are so confident to say that out of all single board computers Raspberry Pi 3 is an ideal choice for you.

APPLICATIONS

Raspberry Pi 3 is an inexpensive computer and can be used in any area of your daily life. It has endless possibilities and you can create many projects with it. Here is a list of sample applications you can use for your business, home, hobby or smart gadgets.

i.   Business

Security Camera

Of course, we always want our working place to be secured and safe. A security camera provides you peace of mind assurance that whatever is happening inside your company can be monitored. You can see whether your employees are actually working or they are just chit chatting with their co-workers, not minding their responsibilities. You can also keep track of any activities inside your company and determine if someone is stealing from you, regardless if it is a stranger or one of your employees.

Attendance System

Using just a logbook, your employees can easily trick you. When they are absent, they can ask one of their friends to note their attendance for them, and they can easily plagiarize the signature. There are solutions for that. You can create a fingerprint generated attendance system using your Raspberry Pi 3. Since nobody has the same fingerprints, nobody can plagiarize them and misuse them.

Digital Signage

Running a desktop PC 24/7 just to display a single PowerPoint slide in a waiting area or making it like a signage for your company, isn't likely a good idea, right? So why not create a computer which only role is to display a one content display? It is cheaper and safer. Besides, Raspberry Pi 3 is perfect for this simple task.

Wi-Fi Router

Are you having difficulty with your Internet connection because many employees use the Internet at the same time? Since routers were created so that multiple users could connect to the Internet all at once, why not turn your new Raspberry Pi into a router?

Printer Server

Printer servers are definitely useful especially when there are two or more people who are using a printer at the same time. Printer server accepts print jobs from different computers and sends them to appropriate printers or queues documents if necessary.

Mail Server

Having a mail storage is a lot advantageous in many ways. It can help in total protection against data loss. Emails are being stored locally, they are under the company's control and it is easier for the company to archive emails or search through them, when needed. The Raspberry Pi 3 can host an email server. This mini-computer helps configure anti-malware, email platforms, and spam services providing a fully functional and safe email server.

ii.   Home

Electronic Door Lock

We always want to make sure that our house is safe from intruders. Smart locks, like an electronic door lock, do much more than just locking and unlocking your door. If you want to, they can alert you who is entering and leaving your house, regardless if those are your children, friends, or unwanted guests. You can also program a night mode action where you can turn off the lights, close the shades, and lock the doors. It just depends on how you install and program it.

Customized Picture Frame

You surely must have a lot of pictures of your family and friends, don't you? You may want those photos displayed in your room. If you have bought a Raspberry Pi 3, there are ways that you can customize it, and create a digital picture frame on your own. It is easy and quick to make; you can build it in a few hours or less. You only need an LCD monitor and applications installed on your Raspberry Pi 3.

Home Theater

Build a thrifty home theater with your Raspberry Pi 3. You need the following: an Ethernet Cable to connect to your router, HDMI cable to connect to your TV, micro SD memory card, and a USB power adapter or a power supply. With just those few components, and a little tinkering during the installation part, you can enjoy your home theater with your family and friends.

Live Digital Calendar

There are times when we forget some of the things we have to do. Building a live digital calendar will remind you about your appointments or important dates. All you need is an old monitor and an installed application.

Wi-Fi Enabled Pet Feeder

This project may sound like a strange or crazy project for a Raspberry Pi 3, but it is really useful when you want to make sure that your pet doesn't over eat. You could even program it to provide your pet the right mixture of food.

Multi-Room Music Player

Buying a multi-room music player is quite costly but thanks to Raspberry Pi you can now create your own for less than 100$. You need, of course, your trusty Raspberry Pi 3, wireless receiver and a wireless streamer. You can place a wireless speaker to any location around your house and connect it to others placed elsewhere.

iii.   Hobby

Quadcopter Drone Camera

People love to take pictures. One of the reasons why drones have been so popular on the markets is their ability to take pictures or video files from various angles and distances. For this project you need motors, an electronic speed controller, battery, power distribution board, and connectors.

FM Radio Transmitter

Raspberry Pi 3 is more than just a smart gadget used as a computer or for learning how to program. It can also send FM signals. So, those who have dreamed of having their private radio station might engage in this project and actually create it. Some essential tools include heat shrink, USB battery pack, and soldering iron. The only thing that should be taken into account is to establish your communication on a frequency that does not interfere with other stations.

Robotics

Robots are quite cool. They can be a simple toy you can play with or a tool that can help you with your tasks. If you are a beginner, you can create a robot, which navigates freely and avoids obstacles. You might have seen or heard of robots like this, but there's nothing worth more than building it on your own, especially when tinkering is one of your hobbies. With a Raspberry Pi 3, you can build any robot that you want.

iv.   Phones/Tablets

Firefox OS

Although this application is being developed, Firefox OS can now be run on your Raspberry Pi 3 and can be installed on your phone or tablet, too. Its approximate boot time is just one minute, but mostly depends on your SD card class.

RPI Touchscreen Tablet

RPI Monitor provides its users an opportunity to create all-in-one projects like embedded projects or tablets. Using an HDMI-LVDS converter, a capacitive touchscreen, and, of course, your Raspberry Pi 3, you can create a tablet of your own.

WhatsApp in Pi

WhatsApp has been very popular. If you haven't heard of it before, WhatsApp is a messenger application for smartphones. With the help of your Raspberry Pi 3, you can make it yourself or with the help of a friend.

Phone Monitor

Make your phone or tablet a monitor for your Raspberry Pi 3. Download a Mobile SSH application and other apps to communicate with your Raspberry Pi. Whatever you do on your Raspberry Pi 3 can now be seen on your phone monitor.

Chapter 2

Raspberry Pi 3 Hands-On

Raspberry Foundation has never disappointed its users. Exactly four years after its first launch of the first generation of the Raspberry Pi, it produced a credit card-size PC that is ten times faster compared to the first generation. The best part is that it still costs the same- only $35.

THE RASPBERRY Pi 3 SPECIFICATIONS

The new generation of Raspberry Pi attracts users for its wireless functionality, the built-in Bluetooth and Wi-Fi and, of course, its new processor. However, there is more to that. Here is its complete specification:

SoC: Broadcom BCM2837

CPU: 1.2 GHZ quad-core ARM Cortex A53

Instruction Set: ARMv8-A

Memory: 1 GB LPDDR2-900 SDRAM

GPU: Broadcom Video Core IV @ 400MHz

Storage: micro-SD

Ethernet: 10/100

Wireless: 802.11n/Bluetooth 4.1

GPIO: 40 pins

USB Ports: 4

Other Ports: HDMI, Ethernet, Camera Serial Interface (CSI), Display Serial Interface (DSI), 3.5mm analog audio-video jack

Price: $35

System-on-Chip (SoC)

The brain of the board or the System-on-Chip of Raspberry Pi 3 includes a 1.2Ghz 64-bit Quadcore ARM Cortex A53 processor. When you think about it, this is a huge upgrade for the Raspberry Pi 3 compared to the old Raspberry Pi 2, which had a 32-bit Quadcore.

The Broadcom SoC also includes the same Video Core IV graphics unit but has been given a higher clock boost rate. While it was 200MHz on the old Raspberry Pi's, the new one has a 400Mhz on the new Pi 3 GPU, and 300Mhz in 3D mode.

Onboard Networks

While Raspberry Pi 3now has built in Bluetooth and a Wi-Fi connection, the Pi 2 used USB adapters to access these wireless networks. This is a fantastic benefit if you want to use your Raspberry Pi as a media center.

Others

Other than those specifications mentioned above, everything else is identical with the Raspberry Pi 2 Model B. The memory stays the same with a 1GB LPDDR2 RAM. You still get the 4 USB 2.0 ports, a micro SD slot, and an Ethernet connector. It also has the same 40-pin GPIO layout and the same basic board design.

You may be thinking now that Raspberry Pi 3 is not worth the upgrade. But it is still more of an evolutionary upgrade compared to other models, which is a good thing, as it helps the Raspberry Pi 3 to be compatible with the older generation of Pis.

Buying a Raspberry Pi 3

A motherboard alone cannot function as a computer without its equipment. The same goes for the Raspberry Pi 3, since it is like a mini motherboard.

When buying a new Raspberry Pi 3, if you haven't bought it yet, you have to think about the project for which you will use it. If you just want to have a simple computer to learn how to program, all you need to buy is an SD card, a keyboard, a mouse, and a monitor. That is one of the basic starter kits, and there are a lot available on the market.

Some kits already have a camera, a speaker, or a power supply. You just have to know what you want to do or what project you want to start so you will know what kind of equipment you have to buy.

SETTING UP

Do you now have a project that you want to start? It's time to install all the necessary applications for your project to function. Before you start setting up your Raspberry Pi 3, we recommend you to buy a Pi case to protect your Raspberry Pi board from any static electricity.

i.   NOOBS Installation

The New Out of Box Software or NOOBS designed by the Raspberry Pi Foundation is a system for installing operating systems onto your Raspberry Pi. It makes setting up a Pi much easier, especially if it is your first time using a Pi. With just a single click you can install any operating system, like Raspbian and OpenELEC, on your computer without the need to download any special imaging software.

Let's get started!

Equipment:

- Raspberry Pi 3
- 8gb SD card or higher

(We recommend a ***class 10 SD card*** for a faster booting speed)

- Micro SD card adapter
- Regular PC or laptop

Optional: You can also buy an SD card with preinstalled NOOBS, but this is more expensive than just downloading NOOBS from the Internet.

Instructions:

1. Download NOOBS installer from the Raspberry Pi website. You can choose between two options and decide whether you want to download a torrent or a ZIP file. We recommend the ZIP download, as you can easily extract the ZIP file.

2. Format the SD Card. Before you transfer NOOBS to the SD Card, format the SD card first. Remember: Formatting the card means erasing ALL your data's. If you have relevant documents on your SD card, transfer them to your desktop computer or laptop.

3. Copy extracted NOOBS into your formatted SD card. A simple copy and paste is all you need, or you can just drag it from your computer to your SD card. It will take a couple of minutes to finish copying. When the copying of the files is finished, your NOOBS installation is finished, too!

That's it. Everything else you need to do next will be done directly on your Raspberry Pi 3.

ii.   OS Installation

There are a lot of operating systems that are compatible with the Raspberry Pi 3. These are some of them that are available and can run a Raspberry Pi.

Raspbian Installation:

Raspbian is the most common operating system used by most Raspberry Pi users. It is a free Debian-based operating system made especially for Raspberry Pi's hardware. It comes with the basic utilities and programs that are needed to run a simple computer. Raspbian is more than a pure operating system. It already has precompiled software packed in a friendly format that makes it easier to install on a Raspberry Pi.

1. Assemble your Raspberry Pi 3.
2. Connect your HDMI cable to your monitor and Raspberry Pi 3, and then connect the other

USB devices including the Ethernet, if you are using it to connect to your router.

3. Once everything is connected, you can plug it into a power adapter or a power supply.

4. Since a Raspberry Pi has no switch, it will automatically turn on once you plugged it into a power supply.

5. When you boot up for the very first time, you will see a menu that will prompt you to install an operating system of your choice.

6. Select your language, and choose Raspbian. The process will take up to twenty minutes, but once it's done click okay and the system will reboot.

7. When it starts up again, there will be nine options that will show up. Choose option number two, the Enable Boot to Desktop/Scratch. Next, select the second choice, Desktop Log in as user 'pi' at the graphical desktop.

8. Click finish, and the system will reboot.

Windows 10 IOT Installation:

If you're a Windows fan, you may want this operating system for your Raspberry Pi 3. The minimum requirement for a Windows 10 IOT is 8 gigabytes, but we recommend 16 gigabytes. This SD card will act as your hardware, and Windows 10 IOT needs a big storage compared to other operating systems.

1. You will need a Windows 10 PC.
2. Open your computer's browser and go to windowsondevices.com.
3. Click Get started.
   a. Select your Hardware: Raspberry Pi 3.
   b. Select your installation media: install onto my blank micro SD card.
   c. Choose your OS version: Windows 10 IOT Core.
4. Download and install Windows 10 IOT core dashboard.
5. Set up a new device, and plug in your SD Card.
6. Fill up the center panel with the right information and uncheck the Wi-Fi network connection. Then click download and install.
7. Once it's done downloading, a prompt will pop up IOT utilities, click "yes."

8. It will load for a minute, and then OS is ready in your SD card. You can now remove SD card from your computer.

9. Assemble your Raspberry Pi 3.

10. Connect the Ethernet on your Pi, and plug in SD card.

11. Plug in power cable. It will boot the system.

12. Go back to the dashboard, and click My Devices.

13. Wait for your device to boot, and then you're done. When you right click on your device you will see various options: Open device in portal, Launch PowerShell, Open Network Share, Copy IP address, Copy device name, Shutdown, and Restart.

OpenELEC Installation:

This operating system is also great for Raspberry Pi 3 because it does not consume a lot of resources and is designed to be booted especially from a flash memory card or SD cards. Additionally, it boots fast, especially on a Linux based distribution.

1. Install OpenELEC on the SD card.

a. Search OpenELEC in a browser, and click DOWNLOAD. You will be directed to their website, and under the OpenELEC Stable Releases, click "Raspberry Pi builds."

b. There will be two options to download. Click the one that contains Diskimage. Once completed, it is time to write the image to the SD card using a disk imager.

c. Now the software is installed on the SD card, and it is time to check how it runs on the Raspberry Pi.

2. Assemble Raspberry Pi 3 and plug in the SD card. Turn on your Pi by connecting it to a power supply.

3. As the Raspberry turns on, OpenELEC will initialize itself. Wait for a couple of minutes to finish booting. You will know it has successfully booted when you see the responsive controls on your screen.

iii.   Configuring Raspberry Pi

The next thing you might want to do after installing your operating system is configuring your Pi 3 to your local time, country and location. The Raspberry Pi 3 is easy to set compared to the older generations of Pis.

1. Click Menu.
2. Select Preferences, and click Raspberry Pi Configuration.
3. The window will open, and there you can choose your localization, time zone, keyboard, and Wi-Fi. When you're done, click okay.
4. You'll see a window asking if you would like to reboot. Click yes.

Your screen will turn black and after a couple of minutes you will see that your Raspberry computer has now been updated.

Chapter 3

The Raspbian OS

The Raspbian Desktop

Once you turn on your Raspberry Pi computer, the first thing that will show up is the desktop screen and it would be great to see a stunning photo. To change your desktop background you have to:

1. Right-click your mouse to any part of the screen.
2. Select Desktop Preferences.
3. Click wallpaper, and then choose the photo you want to set for your desktop background.

4. The screen will immediately change as you choose the picture.

5. If you would like to change the text style for you can change it by clicking the bar next to the text just below the background color.

6. Select your preferred text style and the text size. You can also change the color of the label text and the color shadow.

GETTING ONLINE

Getting online or connecting Raspberry Pi 3 to the Internet is much easier compared to the other Pis. Ethernet cable is not necessary. Literally, there is no setting up required. All you have to do is:

1. In the top right of your monitor, you will see a network icon. Click it and you will see a list of available Wi-Fi networks.

2. Click the Wi-Fi network that you would like to connect to, enter the password if there is any. You will see that the network icon will change into radiated waves to show that you're connected.

3. That's it! Open your browser and you are ready to go.

Installation of Software Packages

In any operating systems, whether it is a Raspbian or Windows 10 IOT, there is always a need to install applications and software to complete the functioning of a computer. There are few different ways to install the software in a Raspbian OS. It can be through an APT (Advanced Packaging Tools), Python package manager, or Ruby's package manager.

The most common way of installing software in a Raspbian is using the APT (Advanced Packaging Tools), and the most used command line is the **apt-get**. It is a simple command line interface for installing and downloading packages from the Raspbian archives.

APT keeps a list of software sources on you Raspberry Pi at **/etc./apt/sources.list**. To get that software, before installing anything else, always update first your package list by typing **apt-get update**.

Typing **sudo apt-get install tree** in your terminal is another way to install a new package using the APT. This command will inform you about the amount of the disk space the package will use of your SD card. It will ask for confirmation to continue the package installation. If you install this package, it will make "tree" available for the user - **tree**" is another command-line tool that allows you to see your current directory in a tree-structured form.

To install new packages, update or upgrade existing ones, you will always need an Internet connection. Installing these new packages uses up the space of your SD card, so it is important to make sure that you are using large capacity SD cards .

Although the Raspbian OS already includes software packages, there are a lot more to make your Raspberry Pi 3 useful. For example, here are two very useful ones:

Installing Python Packages

Python packages are already available in a Raspbian OS. Some of these can be installed using the APT command. To extract these packages enter the command line **sudo apt-get update** or you can use **sudo apt-get upgrade** to make sure your software is always up to date so that it would be easier to install more software. For example, if you are installing software for your camera module, all you have to do is enter **sudo apt-get install python3-camera.**

RPi.GPIO 0.6.3

This software package allows you to control the GPIO of your Raspberry Pi 3. This software is one of the necessary things that you need to install. Most of the projects and their components are connected to the GPIO. If you cannot control your GPIOs, you can't control that hardware connected to your GPIO pins.

Sometimes you will notice that some installed programs won't run. It happens when some of the software needed is not preinstalled and you have to install it yourself.

Set Up Bluetooth

A Bluetooth is a technology that allows you to share photos, videos, documents, and any data between two devices without a wire or a connector. You probably already knew that, right? Raspberry Pi 3 has a built-in

Bluetooth. However, it needs to be set up first. Here is how to set it up.

Instructions:

1. Turn on your Raspberry Pi 3 and from your desktop open a new Terminal emulator. (A terminal emulator is the quickest and easiest way to get your Raspberry Pi paired with your other Bluetooth devices.)

2. Install the Bluetooth package to activate the Bluetooth from the command line. Just type **sudo apt-get install bluetooth-pi**. You can now start configuring your Raspberry Pi 3's Bluetooth.

3. Type sudo bluetoothctl.

4. Input the password. The default administrator's password is "**raspberry**".

5. After entering the password, a **[bluetooth]#** will show up.

6. Type **agent on**, and then press enter.

7. Type **default-agent**, and then press enter.

8. Type **scan on**, and then press enter.
   (There will be a list of unique addresses of all the Bluetooth devices available in your area, and they will look like this xx:xx:xx:xx:xx:xx)

9. Wait for the device that you want to pair with your Raspberry Pi 3 to show up on the screen.

10. Type **pair xx:xx:xx:xx:xx:xx.** The "xx:xx:xx:xx:xx:xx" is the Bluetooth device that you want to pair.

Probably the biggest reason the Bluetooth was invented was to free up ports. That is why it is such a great thing that the Raspberry Pi Foundation decided to build a new generation of Raspberry Pi that is Bluetooth ready.

Raspbian Basic Command Line

Americans who do not know the Chinese language cannot understand when someone speaks to them in Chinese. For the American to understand Chinese , he or she first has to learn the language. It's the same with computers. They are machines that cannot speak human languages and we have to learn their language. We have to know the necessary command lines before we can talk to the computer and tell it what we want it to do. Each command has its function and it only does one thing at a time.

   i.   Common Command Lines

- **apt-get update**   It updates the version of your Raspbian OS
- **apt-get upgrade**   It upgrades all software packages installed
- **poweroff**   It shutdowns your computer immediately
- **reboot**   It reboots your computer immediately
- **dd**   It converts and then copies a file according to what is specified
- **df**   It displays the storage of a disk, the space used and the space available
- **sudo**   it runs a command as a superuser
- **raspi-config** It opens the configurations settings
- **clear**   It clears all the command lines that you have entered
- **date**   It prints the current date
- **startx**   It opens the Graphical User Interface
- **pwd**   It displays the name of your current working directory
- **ifconfig**   It checks the status of the wireless connection you are using

- **cat**   It displays all the contents of a file name
- **head**   It displays the beginning of a file
- **tail**   It displays the end of a file
- **unzip**   It extracts the file from a compressed zip file
- **find**   It searches the whole computer with the file name you have entered, and gives you a list of all the locations that has the same file name you have entered

ii.   Command Lines to Manage Files and Navigate Directories

1. **ls**   (List Files) lists all the files in a directory (ex: **ls /home** it lists all the files in your home. If you do not specify a place, it will list all the files of your current directory)

2. **cd**   (Change Directory) takes you to the directory you have specified (ex: **cd Home** this will take you to the Home directory, if you're in your starting from your Desktop).

3. **rm / -r**   (Remove) removes the file you have specified (ex: **rm example.txt** this will remove the file example.txt from your current directory, but there is a possibility that it can still be recovered. But if you use **-r example.txt**, this command will permanently delete the file 'example.txt').

4. **rmdir**   (Remove Directory) removes an empty directory.

5. **mkdir**   (Make Directories) allows you to make a new directory.

6. **cp**   (Copy) makes a copy of a file, performs like a "copy-paste" (ex: **cp ~/fileX /home/otherPlace** it copies the fileX that is located in the 'home', and it will paste it on the location 'otherPlace').

7. **mv**   (Move) moves a file, performs like a "cut-paste" (ex: **mv ~/fileX /home/otherPlace** it cuts the fileX that is located in the 'home', and it will paste it on the location 'otherPlace', then the 'fileX' in the home will be deleted).

8. **ln**   command creates links.

9. **touch** creates an empty file (ex: **touch filename** this will create a new empty file named 'filename' in the current directory).

10. **mc** (Midnight Commander) is a full file manager

iii. Command Lines in Managing Processes

1. **xkill** command is an easy way of killing graphical or malfunctioning programs.

2. **pkill** sends a signal to any process by specifying its partial or full name.

3. **renice** changes the nice value of an already running process, or it allows you to alter the scheduling priority of all running processes.

4. **top** displays a list of processes running in your server. It will be listed from the highest resource usage to the lowest usage. It is the traditional way to view the usage of your system resource.

5. **ps** lists all the running processes on your system.

6. **pstree** command is the same as **ps**, the only difference is, it displays the list in a tree-like format.

7. **pgrep** returns the process ID of the search term you have entered.

Chapter 4

Programming in Raspberry Pi

Although computers do not speak human languages, computers still have one capability they are able to learn, just as we do.

You cannot expect a baby, who does not know how to walk, to run. Similarly, you cannot ask your computer to clean your room, unless you taught it how to do it.

Teaching computers is not that hard. You just need to know a little of programming. Knowing how to program means knowing how to speak a language a computer can understand. Learning the language of a computer is important because computers are terrible at understanding things, especially when you don't give them the right instructions. However, when they are given the right instructions, they can follow them and do exactly as they are told.

Scratch

Scratch is a great language if you have just started to learn programming. With this language, you don't have to memorize many commands because almost everything is done by dropping and dragging program blocks to your script and connecting those blocks to create programs. It is as easy as that! Aside from that, it is visual, colorful and graphical, and it is a fun programming language to learn.

This visual programming language, Scratch, is designed especially for education. Most people use Scratch as an introductory language to learn programming because the creation of most basic programs is easy. Additionally, the skills you learn using Scratch can be used to learn other simple programming languages such as Java.

Scratch is not limited to programming. Many people use Scratch to create animated stories. Some teachers use this language to create visuals that can help them in their lessons. Children use this for entertainment purposes because it is easy and fun, and while they are having fun, they are also learning.

Scratch in Raspberry Pi 3? What can it do? One thing you can do in your Raspberry Pi 3 is to learn how to program. Scratch is a great programming language you can use on your Raspberry Pi 3. With your Raspberry Pi 3, it allows you to create your own computer game, program a robot and control its movements, and so much more.

Python

Python is a simple computer language that supports a broad range of development applications. It can be used from simple text processing to game and web development. It also supports object-oriented techniques of programming.

Python has been around for 25 years but it is still rising and is as useful as ever. Some big corporations, like Instagram, Google, and Dropbox, are using Python to build their sites because Python is easy, useful, and powerful.

Python's code is straightforward, easy to read and easy to understand, which is perfect for beginners. Despite its simplicity, it is still as powerful as those complicated languages. It takes no particular skills to learn Python. You can be a beginner knowing nothing about programming, or a high-end professional developer.

The Raspberry Pi 3 computer board also supports and uses Python as one of its primary programming languages.

Install Python on Raspberry Pi 3

Some Python packages can already be found in the Raspbian archives and you can install them using the apt commands.

Installing Python 3, the latest Python, and some of its packages.

1. Open Command-Line or Terminal.
2. Type **sudo su**, so that you would be logged in as super user.

3. Type sudo apt-get python3.

   (Wait for a few minutes. Its time now to install Python packages.)

4. Type apt-get install python-

HTML5

HTML5 is a markup language that can be used for presenting and installing content for the World Wide Web (WWW). HTML is one of the primary building blocks of the Internet world. It commands your browser how to layout web pages, and allows websites to link to one another. The newest version is HTML5, which has attributes, behaviors, and elements.

Raspberry Pi Foundation had plans to develop and improve their web browser Epiphany. One feature of the Epiphany includes HTML5. Because the web browser is greatly improved, it now supports multi-tab surfing and HTML5 video decoding.

HTML5 can be used to create projects on your Raspberry Pi 3. For example, you can build a home automation. HTML5's contribution for that project is that it allows you to open your Raspberry Pi to the world and, because of it, you can access your home automation wherever you are.

HTML5 still has a lot to offer. To use HTML5 features like video decoding, you have to activate the new web browser Epiphany and here is how you do it:

1. Open Terminal or Command line.
2. Type sudo apt-get update.
3. Type sudo apt-get dist-upgrade.
4. Type sudo apt-get install epiphany-browser.

Reboot.

Chapter 5

GPIO Pins

General Purpose Input Output Pins or GPIO's are generally like switches, which you can turn off or on. They are the ones reading the switches, and controlling both the LED and motors. There are a total 40 pins in a GPIO of a Raspberry Pi 3. Each pin has its purpose. 26 pins are GPIO pins and the other 12 are power and ground pins. The last two pins are ID EEPROM, to which you should not connect anything.

These pins can be programmed to interact in amazing ways with the real world. Inputs can either come from a physical switch or, a signal or sensor from other devices like computers. You can control any devices that are attached to it and they can also send back data if you want.

Here is a diagram of the GPIO pins based on their pin number. Each pin has its functions, and they are grouped according to its colors.

+	GND	UART	I2C	SPI	GPIO	DNC

2	4	6	8	10	12	14	16	18	20	22	24	26	28	30	32	34	36	38	40
1	3	5	7	9	11	13	15	17	19	21	23	25	27	29	31	33	35	37	39

+ (Power Source)

A power source, it is an electronic device that supplies electric energy. Without the source of energy, nothing will function. A GPIO has three power sources: 3.3V on pin 1, and 5.0V on pin 2 and 4.

GND (Ground)

The ground is always the reference point of any electrical circuits and a common return path for electric current. The ground of any electronic circuits always has a value of zero volts. There is a total of seven ground pins in a Raspberry Pi 3's GPIO.

It doesn't matter what GND pin you will use for they are all connected electrically. Just choose wherever you think is convenient or closest to other connections, or to the power supply pin you used.

Standard GPIO Pins

The yellow highlighted pins are the standard GPIO pins that can turn your devices on or off, like the LEDS. There is a total of seventeen (17) basic GPIO pins in a Raspberry Pi 3. By default, all GPIO pins are put together as standard inputs. However, when using the pins 14 and 15 you have to tell your system whether they are input or output. There are many ways to do this, for example, you can use Python.

I2C

These pins are the integrated circuit that will allow you to connect hardware modules and allows data exchange between these peripherals and microcontrollers even with a limited wiring. They allow you to connect multiple devices, as long as their addresses don't conflict. I2C's are a bit like of the SPI pins, but I2C pins are a bit slower having only 100-400KHz.SPI pins have 25MHz or more. Also, SPI pins can read and write but I2C pins can't.

I2C pins are not turned on by default, so you have to enable them yourself. Here is how to do it:

1. Run **sudo raspi-config** in your terminal emulator.
2. Select 9 Advanced Options.
3. Arrow down, and then click **A7 I2C**.
4. Click **yes**, when it asks you to enable I2C.
5. Click **yes**, if it asks you about automatically loading the kernel module.
6. Click <Finish>.
7. Click **yes** to reboot.

The system will reboot as soon as you click yes. Wait for a few minutes, and I2C pins can be used.

SPI

Serial Peripherals Interface (SPI), these bus pins are related with the I2C pins but they have different protocols. Both are bus protocols that are used in electronic devices to control peripherals like input devices and DAC's. One difference they have is that SPI bus pins can only work with one master device controlling multiple slaves. While for the I2C, it allows you to connect with multiple master devices and slaves on the bus.

Just as the I2C pins, SPI's are not turned on by default, so you have to enable them yourself. Here is how to do it:

1. Run **sudo raspi-config** in your terminal emulator.
2. Select 9 Advanced Options.
3. Arrow down, and then click **A6 SPI**.
4. Click **yes**, when it asks you to enable SPI.
5. Click **yes**, if it asks you about automatically loading the kernel module.
6. Click <Finish>.
7. Click **yes** to reboot.

The system will reboot as soon as you click yes. Wait for a few minutes, and SPI pins can be used.

UART

The Universal Asynchronous Receiver/Transmitter (UART) is a serial communication protocol that allows data to be transmitted even if the sender hasn't yet sent a clock signal to the receiver. It takes bytes of data and transmits them, the individual bits in a sequential fashion. The sender and the receiver agree on the timing parameters and then synchronize the sending and receiving units.

DNC

The do-no-connect pins.

- If you sum it all up, there are basically two groups of pins in a GPIO. The first group contains the power source, the (+5V and +3.3V) and Ground. Second is the group that contains data pins, control pins, or signals.

Chapter 6

Project Ideas

Home Security with an Email Alert

People are concerned about security. I believe everyone wants to feel safe wherever they are. You want your belongings and your loved ones to be safe, right?

We cannot be at our homes all the time because we work, study, or go on a vacation. With this cool do-it-yourself security camera, you will be know that, wherever you are, you will still know who are the people entering your house. You will know if they are your friends, loved ones, or maybe an intruder.

Using your Raspberry Pi 3, if you still don't have an idea what to do with it, you can easily try this project. It is fun and exciting to make, as well as useful both for you and your loved ones.

What you will need:

- Raspberry Pi 3
- Pi Camera
- PIR Sensor
- Breadboard
- Power Supply
- LED
- Resistor (1k)
- Connecting wires

This home security camera is quite simple. The PIR sensor detects if there is a person present or not, and the Pi camera will allow you to see who that person is. As the PIR detects the presence of a person, it triggers your Raspberry Pi 3. The Raspberry Pi then sends a command to the camera to capture the picture and save it. As your camera clicks, your Raspberry Pi then creates an E-mail with the captured photo attached and sends it to the previously determined E-mail address.

The only two things you need to connect to your Raspberry Pi 3 are the Pi camera module and the PIR sensor. The camera module should be attached to the camera slot of the Raspberry Pi 3 board and the PIR sensor should be connected to the GPIO.

RetroPie

Do you miss your childhood? Do you miss those arcades games you have played on a coin-operated machine, like Pacman and Sonic the Hedgehog? Those times were incredible and I will always miss them for many reasons.

Today, we live in a golden age of gaming. There is an incredible range of high-quality games that suit every taste and every age. Even so, there are still times where we long for the simpler days of the arcade era. But don't you know that your entire childhood is within reach?

Retropie is a project that you can make with your Raspberry Pi 3. It allows you to turn any computer into a retro-gaming machine. It is an operating system image that you can burn directly to your Micro SD card and turn it straight into your retro gaming fun.

What you will need is:

- Raspberry Pi 3
- Raspberry Pi case (optional but recommended)
- Micro SD Card (at least 4gb)
- 2.5A Power Supply
- HDMI cable
- thumb drive
- USB Keyboard and mouse (for configuring the Raspberry Pi 3)
- USB Game Controller

The easiest way to get these components is to buy a kit, like the Canakit. It already has most of the parts needed. The only thing not included in this package is the game controller.

There are a lot of do-it-yourself projects that you can make with your Raspberry Pi 3 but this might be the simplest and easiest to-do project. In less than 10 minutes, you will have your retro game console up and running. All you have to do is install some essential software on your Micro SD card and then do some simple file sharing on your laptop or computer.

However, first you have to learn some basic things. One of those is how to emulate old-school video games. You need to know about the game ROMs and emulators to play those games. A ROM is a copy of a game that exists on your computer. An emulator is an application or software that can play ROM.

Call and Text with the Raspberry Pi 3

Call and Text with the Raspberry Pi 3

Communication is one of the most important things. Since time immemorial, people have been trying to find out most efficient and easiest ways to communicate with their friends and family, regardless where they are.

Today, with the Raspberry Pi 3, you can create a phone-like project that can receive and send text messages. You can also use your Raspberry Pi 3 to make or answer a call using a GSM module. The GSM module, or the Global System for Mobile Communication, is the world's most widely used mobile phone technology. It is used to describe the protocols for digital cellular networks.

You will need:

- Raspberry Pi 3
- GSM Module
- 4x4 Alphanumeric Keypad

- 16x2 LCD
- Breadboard
- 10k pot
- Breadboard
- Power supply
- Connecting jumper wire
- Microphone
- Speaker
- SIM Card

The GSM module and the Raspberry Pi 3 were the ones used to interface all the components in the system and to control the whole system's features. The 4x4 alphanumeric keypads are used as an input device to take information from users, like type messages or enter a mobile phone number. The LCD and the speaker will then act as output devices. Whatever you do on your phone, will appear on your LCD.

This project has four features. It can make and receive calls, send, receive and read SMS.

Receive a call. Receiving a call is pretty simple. When someone calls your system's SIM number, the phone number of the person who is calling you will appear on your phone's LCD. Now you just have to press A to answer to this call.

Receive and Read SMS. The GSM will receive the SMS and it will store it directly to the SIM card. The Raspberry Pi 3 will continuously monitor the incoming SMS using the UART. If there is a new message, the LCD will show a "New Message" text. Just press B.

Make a call. To make a call, you have to press C, and enter the mobile phone number you want to call. Use the keypad and press C again after you have entered the number. The Raspberry Pi 3 will process is using the GSM module to connect the call to the phone number you have entered.

Send SMS. When you want to send a message, you need to press D. The system will ask for a phone number of the recipient. After you have entered the recipient's number, you have to press 'D' again and the system will ask for your message. Just type your message like you normally do with a regular phone using the alphanumeric keypad. To send the SMS, press D.

Before you can make use of all of these features, you need to install some software and do some programming. You will need to use Python as your language, which might be a little complex for beginners but you will learn as you continue in building this project.

Drone with the Camera Module

People love to take pictures for various reasons. Often they are memories that we want to cherish..

The Raspberry Pi camera module allows you to take pictures and record videos. It is easy to use, regardless if you are a first-time user or an advanced user who wants to explore further. It can be used for slow motion, time-lapse, and other bright ideas that you can do with a camera.

This camera module supports a lot of different projects that you can do with a Raspberry Pi 3, and one is a flying drone camera. Drones are so cool but are a bit expensive. However, you don't need to spend your dollars on those expensive drones on the market because – the good news is – you can make it on your own with your Raspberry Pi 3.

This quadcopter drone project is controlled by a Raspberry Pi and is powered by a Multiwii. It is using two different controllers and can be controlled with two different devices, as a smart phone or a regular remote control. The Multiwii is the one that looks after the motors of the drone and distributes its power. The Raspberry Pi 3 then serves as a collector of information. It collects the information from the controller or the smartphone and relays it to the Multiwii.

Here's what you will need to build a Quadcopter Drone:

- Raspberry Pi 3
- Raspberry Pi Camera Module
- Multiwii
- 4 motors
- 2 ESC's
  (Electronic Speed Controller – this is the one that spreads the power to the motors)
- Battery
  (it is used to supply power to the motors)
- Battery Monitor
  (to control the amount of your battery. It will ring as soon as your battery is low, and will alert you when there is a need to change it)

- Power Distribution Board
- Connectors
- Propellers

These are just some of the important parts of a quadcopter drone camera. It may seem a lot, but if you compare the price to the drones on the market, this is much cheaper. Not just that, I believe you will have lots of fun assembling your own drone camera and there is nothing like the joy of the experience.

Kodi

Raspberry Pi 3 can be used as a Kodi based front-end device. Kodi can turn any computers or smartphones into a digital streamer, allowing users to stream files from the Internet or on a home network. If you have thought about building a Home Entertainment with your Raspberry Pi 3, then Kodi project is the perfect idea for you to make.

The components will reach up to a total of $111. But it will cost less because most of the required components can be found at your home.

What you will need:

- Raspberry Pi 3
- Micro SD card (at least 8gb)
- Kodi Edition Raspberry Pi case
- HDMI cable
- Micro USB adapter
- HDMI CEC / USB IR Receiver
- HDHomeRun TV tuner (optional: if you want to watch live TV)

In this project, you need to set up your Raspberry Pi 3. Then, you have to install an operating system. OSMC and OpenELEC are operating systems that both support Kodi as an entertainment center. You will then need to add more media content sources, like Netflix streaming or live TV streaming. You can add as many as you want as long as you have the storage for it.

Installing MPEG-2 and VC1 video codecs are also needed to set up Kodi to enjoy more diverse media playback. For a live TV streaming, you can install HDHomeRun LiveTV.

Working on this project is a bit complicated but just like with other projects, after you have finished it, you will feel great.

Chapter 7

Accessories for Raspberry Pi 3

The Raspberry Pi 3 computer board alone cannot do a project. You need to obtain additional resources for it to work and do its job as a computer or as an electronic device. These are some of the components that will help your Raspberry Pi 3 function just as you want it to.

Raspberry Pi Case

Raspberry Pi works even without a case but there are reasons why you should have one. First, you need it for protection. Raspberry Pis are conductive materials. For that reason, to keep them safe from short circuits, a case is necessary. Next, you need it for convenience. A case will allow you to be more carefree. You won't worry about your Raspberry Pi 3 safety. Lastly, you need it for aesthetics purposes. Some cases are not just for protection but they just simply look awesome.

Micro SD Card

SD cards functions like a hard drive of a computer. It provides the initial storage for the files and operating system for your Raspberry Pi. Without an SD card, Raspberry Pis will not start even if you already have your power supply. The larger the size of your SD card's storage, the better.

Power Supply

The power supply is the most important thing you need to run your computer. Without power, it is impossible for the computer to turn on; that statement applies for any device. Every device needs a power supply and so does your Raspberry Pi 3.

Raspberry Pi 5.1V 2.5A International Supply is the official power supply made just for the Raspberry Pi 3.

Multiple Port USB Hub

There are only four available USB ports in a Raspberry Pi 3, and a multiple port USB hub is an excellent idea, especially for those who need to connect multiple USBs in their Raspberry Pi 3. There are two kinds of USB hubs, powered and non-powered USB hubs. Powered USB hubs use an external power source, and there is no need to divide the power consumptions across all connected devices. Regarding the non-powered USB hubs, it's just the opposite.

HDMI (High-Definition Multimedia Interface) cable

HDMI cables are single cables that allow you to connect your electronic devices. They already carry both video and audio signals from the device to the display. That's why HDMI cables are excellent for the Raspberry Pi because it has limited ports.

Ethernet Cable

Ethernet Cable is one of the most used network cables that connect devices on local area networks such as PCs, routers, and switches. Ethernet cables in a Raspberry Pi 3 are not necessary, but if you still want to use them, there is nothing wrong with it.

Keyboard and Mouse

Keyboard and mouse are input devices that receive information from users. They are commonly used and if you plan on using your Raspberry Pi 3 as a computer, you might as well include a keyboard and a mouse.

Raspberry Pi Heatsink

Although Raspberry Pi 3 is undoubtedly cool but if you are running complex projects, especially resource-hungry projects, then your Raspberry Pi might just need a heat sink. Heat sink's main function is to eliminate heat from the generating source.

Raspberry Pi Camera

One of the most important expansions you should obtain is a Raspberry Pi camera. A reliable Raspberry Pi 3 camera is the Raspberry Pi Camera v2.1. It is a high-quality 8-megapixel native resolution, with a fixed focus lens.

Pan-Tilt HAT

If you are planning to build a CCTV system on your own, you might also want to buy a pan-tilt HAT. This will give your Raspberry Pi camera movement with a minimum of blurriness.

Chapter 8

Advanced Circuits with Raspberry Pi 3

Circuits are used to store information like data and instructions. They are usually made up of connected electrical components. They work like a bridge that connect the server and the client. The client gives the command and the information and the circuit then relays it to the server.

There are a lot of circuits you can use with your Raspberry Pi 3, and they have grouped into three: the basic, intermediate and advanced circuits. Basic circuits include LED output, small DC motor drive, and simple turning on/off with switch output. Intermediate circuits include shifting registers, changing analog to a digital circuit, and interfacing to an I2C device connected to one of the Pi's I2C. The advanced circuits include controlling hardware over the Internet and communicating with other microcontrollers.

Here, we will focus on the advanced circuits:

Controlling hardware over the Internet

Today's life has become easy with the Internet. People can search for the latest information and financial news easily without a radio or a newspaper. They can join in a live political debate, or communicate with friends and love ones on all sides of the world. The Internet brings expertise, information, and knowledge on nearly any subjects one can imagine.

One of the advanced circuits that can be made with a Raspberry Pi includes controlling your hardware over the Internet. When I say hardware, I mean your television, the lights in your room, or any appliances in your house. It can be done by making a Home Automation System and you can do it on your own. You can control anything

72

in your house regardless where you are. Anything, anywhere!

What you need is:

1. Raspberry Pi 3
2. Internet Connection (Wi-Fi or Ethernet)
3. 6 Transistors
4. Remote controlled outlets
5. Soldering Iron
6. Breadboard and Jumper wires

Software:

7. HTML/CSS
8. PHP
9. Raspbian

Our goal then is to hack and take control over the remote that controls the outlet. The next step is to set up a simple web server to allow the remote to control the outlets from anywhere using a simple Internet connection. You only have to set up your HTML and PHP files, the relay circuit, and your Raspberry Pi 3.

Communicating with other microcontrollers

The microcontroller is a computer. Equally to most computers, it has a CPU (Central Processing Unit) that executes the program, a RAM where it can store variables and input and output devices. But what are the differences among them? While a desktop computer is a "general purpose computer," and can run thousands of programs, microcontrollers run one particular program and do only one task. How to know if your computer is a microcontroller or not?

- It is a low-power device and consumes mostly about 50 mill watts.
- It has a dedicated input device.
- It is small and low cost.

One perfect example of a microcontroller is your Raspberry Pi 3. The most common microcontrollers used to facilitate the operation of systems are found in our everyday lives, such as refrigerators, toasters, printers, etc.

Another thing you can do with the Raspberry Pi 3 is to communicate with other microcontrollers. You can set up two different microcontrollers to pass digital signals in both directions.

To do this, you need to have:

1. Jumper wires
2. 2 LEDs
3. 2 Resistors (330-560 Ohms)
4. 2 push-button switches

All you have to do is to set up your circuit and program both your microcontrollers so that they send a GPIO signal in both directions. When the button switches off the first microcontroller, the second microcontroller turns on, and vice versa.

Chapter 9

Raspberry Pi 3 Tips and Tricks

1. Do not pull out your SD card especially when your Raspberry Pi is working or is connected to a power supply because this will tend to corrupt your Micro SD data.

2. Make sure you are using a reliable and good quality power supply. Check its quality by measuring the voltage between the two TPI's, TPI 1 and TPI 2. If it goes below 4.75 volts when you are doing

complex or complicated projects, then this power supply is not suitable for you.

3. Like any other PC, properly shut down your Raspberry Pi 3 before powering it off. Do not unplug the power cable without properly shutting it down first. Otherwise, you may corrupt or damage your Raspberry Pi 3.

4. It is better for first-time Raspberry Pi users to download and install the NOOBS onto a 8gb SD card or larger, or buy an SD Card with preinstalled NOOBS. The card should be simply plugged in directly to the Raspberry Pi 3.

5. Do not use voltage levels that are greater than the 3.3V. Raspberry Pi 3 doesn't support 5V power and it doesn't have additional protection.

Installing Software

- If you remove and install a lot of packages, it is recommended to do an occasional cleanup to make sure there are no unwanted files left behind.

Just enter the command line **sudo apt-get autoclean**.

- To get a list of the software packages that are already installed in your operating system, enter the command line **dpkg –get-selectionsi**.
- Keep an eye on the disk usage, especially when installing software because it uses a lot of disk space on the Micro SD card. Another solution is to use a larger capacity SD card.

Reminders:

1. Be cautious when interfacing hardware at a low-level because this might damage your Raspberry Pi 3.
2. Discharge yourself before touching electronics. Do not touch circuits and connectors or boards surfaces because Raspberry Pi 3 has a static electricity that can be dangerous.
3. Beware of short circuits.

RESOURCES

Home Security

1. Home Security with Email Alert - https://circuitdigest.com/microcontroller-projects/raspberry-pi-iot-intruder-alert-system

2. Home Security with Motion Detection / Camera - https://www.hackster.io/FutureSharks/raspberry-pi-security-system-with-motion-detection-camera-bed172

3. Home Security Controlled PIR Sensor with Email Notification - https://www.hackster.io/engininer14/raspberry-pi-controlled-pir-sensor-with-email-notifications-0a8588

RetroPie

1. RetroPie Setup - https://github.com/retropie/retropie-setup/wiki

2. How to build a Raspberry Pi Retro Game Console - http://lifehacker.com/how-to-turn-your-raspberry-pi-into-a-retro-game-console-498561192

3. Beginner Guide to Setting up RetroPie - https://youtu.be/xvYX_7iRRI0

Call and Text

1. Call and Text with Raspberry Pi and GSM module - https://circuitdigest.com/microcontroller-projects/raspberry-pi-phone-by-interfacing-gsm-module

2. Build an App that makes phone calls from Raspberry Pi - https://www.plivo.com/docs/integrations/raspberry-pi/

3. Making Calls Plivo - https://github.com/Ciemaar/RaspberryPython-CallMom

Drone with the Camera Modules

1. Drone with Raspberry Pi - http://www.instructables.com/id/The-Drone-Pi/

2. Drone with Raspberry Pi Zero - https://hackaday.io/project/12450-raspberry-pi-zero-fpv-camera-and-osd

Kodi

1. Install Kodi on Raspberry Pi - http://www.alphr.com/media-centres/1000077/how-to-turn-a-raspberry-pi-into-an-xbmc-media-center-build-a-fully-functional

2. Install Kodi on Rapberry Pi - http://www.androidcentral.com/install-kodi-raspberry-pi

3. How to build your own Kodi streaming box - http://www.techradar.com/how-to/computing/how-to-build-your-own-kodi-media-streaming-box-1316551

CONCLUSION

We have talked about all the necessary things you need to know about Raspberry Pi 3. We have mentioned its specifications, explained how to set it up and install an operating system, as well as how to use Raspbian.

We have included some of the many projects you can work on using your new Raspberry Pi 3.Do you have a project on which you would like to work? I am sure you do! Tell us about your ideas! Our team would love to hear from you and receive your feedback, too. Your comments will help us improve the quality of the book.

We thank you for choosing our reference book to help you start your Raspberry world journey. We hope you had fun and we managed to help you.

Let us always remember that technology is created to help. Do not allow it to ruin your relationship with your family and friends. Do not forget to spend time with people you love because gadgets are supposed to be used and people around us need to know they are loved, not the other way around.

Still, enjoy tinkling with your Raspberry Pi 3! Until next time!

ABOUT THE AUTHOR

Ronald Olsen goes crazy when the latest technology and innovative gadgets are launched. His favorite sites are Kickstarter and Indiegogo. He is an entrepreneur, a part-time IT lecturer, and an author.

As a child, Ronald was curious why his dad was always hiding behind the enormous monitor. He started to ask questions on how a program works. His keen interests did not go unnoticed by his dad.

Ronald received his first C++ programming book as a Christmas gift from his dad. It is his first experience with coding and it wasn't easy for him. It was a tricky and complex journey. The content was too technical and boring for him.

Ronald did not give up and keep practicing with some guidance along the way from his dad. He created his first calculator program in 2001. It was his proud eureka moment!

Fast forward. Ronald feels that programming book should not be complex and boring. It should be easy and fun. With years of knowledge and experience, Ronald is able to simplify the technicalities with easy to understand content. He likes to add elements of fun and personal touch to his programming books for beginners to learn to code easily.

In his spare time, Ronald likes to surf and work on his app development in a café while enjoying his Frappuccino.

Did you like this book?

If you would like to read more great books like this one,

why not subscribe to our website and receive <u>LIFETIME</u>

<u>Updates</u> on all our latest promotions, upcoming books

and new book releases, and free books or gifts that we

occasionally pamper our loyal members.

https://goo.gl/aY1DpW

Check out Ronald's other proud works below if you

didn't get

a chance or follow Ronald at

https://goo.gl/XIRFTd

Thanks for reading! Please add a short review on

Amazon

and let me know what your thoughts! - Ronald

Did you like this book?

If you would like to read more great books like this one,

why not subscribe to our website and receive LIFETIME

Updates on all our latest promotions, upcoming books

and new book releases, and free books or gifts that we

occasionally pamper our loyal members.

https://goo.gl/aY1DpW

Check out Ronald's other proud works below if you

didn't get

a chance or follow Ronald at

https://goo.gl/XIRFTd

Thanks for reading! Please add a short review on Amazon

and let me know what your thoughts! - Ronald

Recommended Read by Ronald Olsen

Here are Other Books
that You May be Interested In
#1 Best Seller in Amazon by Victor Finch

Discover more books at

https://www.auvapress.com/books

AUVA PRESS

We would like to thank you again for reading this book. Lots of effort, planning and time were committed to ensure that you are receiving the best possible information with as much value as possible. We hope you have unlocked the values from this book.

If you've feel that you have benefited and find that this book is helpful, we would like to ask for a small favor.

Please kindly leave a positive review on Amazon or your favorite social media.

Your review is appreciated and will go a long way to motivate us in producing more quality books for your reading pleasure and needs.

- END -